Treasury of Girls' Stories

Featuring The Magic Dancing Shoes, The Princess Puzzle and The Princess and the Peasant Girl

igloobooks

The Magic Dancing Shoes

Annabel wanted nothing more than to be able to dance. Her grandmother had been a very famous dancer and Annabel would spend hours looking at all the old photographs and trophies at her grandparents' house. She would imagine herself on stage, in the spotlight, dancing in front of a huge crowd.

But no matter how hard she tried, Annabel couldn't make her feet do what she wanted them to. She watched enviously as the other girls in her class twirled across the floor. "Why am I so clumsy?" she would sigh.

One day, Annabel was visiting her grandparents' house, when her grandma took her aside. "How are the dancing lessons going, Annabel?" she asked.
"Oh Nana, I just can't do it!" cried Annabel. "I'm always practicing, but I just can't get it right."
"Of course you can," laughed her grandmother. "You just have to believe you can do it. Now wait there a moment, I have something for you."

Nana came back with a cardboard box and handed it to Annabel.
"Well, open it," she laughed.

Inside the box, hidden beneath crumpled brown paper, was the prettiest, most delicate music box Annabel had ever seen. She opened it to find a little fairy ballerina spinning around to a simple, elegant melody.
"It's beautiful Nana! Thank you!" cried Annabel.

"It belonged to me when I was a little girl," said Nana. "You must promise to take very good care of it. That music box is much more special than you think."

Annabel wasn't really sure what she meant by this, but she gave her a big hug and then ran off to show her parents the wonderful gift.

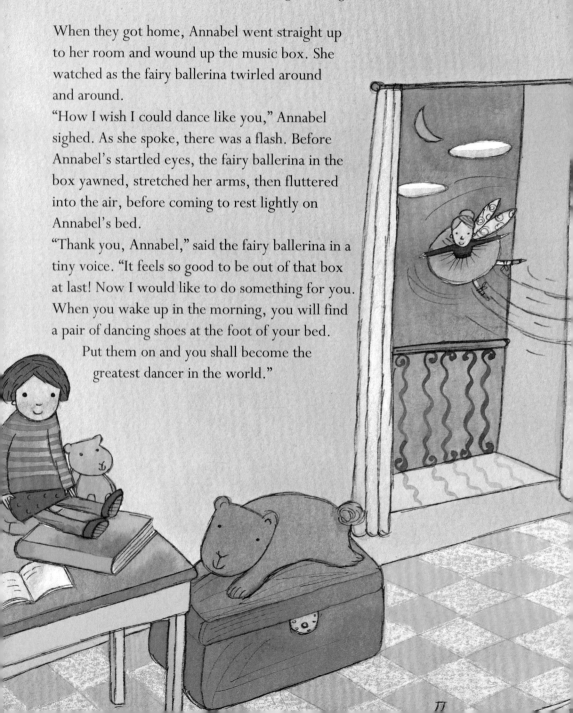

When they got home, Annabel went straight up
to her room and wound up the music box. She
watched as the fairy ballerina twirled around
and around.

"How I wish I could dance like you," Annabel
sighed. As she spoke, there was a flash. Before
Annabel's startled eyes, the fairy ballerina in the
box yawned, stretched her arms, then fluttered
into the air, before coming to rest lightly on
Annabel's bed.

"Thank you, Annabel," said the fairy ballerina in a
tiny voice. "It feels so good to be out of that box
at last! Now I would like to do something for you.
When you wake up in the morning, you will find
a pair of dancing shoes at the foot of your bed.

Put them on and you shall become the
greatest dancer in the world."

Without another word, the fairy flew into the air and out of the open window. Annabel could hardly believe what she had seen.

"My imagination must be playing tricks on me," she thought, as she climbed into bed that night. She knew that fairies didn't really exist. And as for a pair of magic shoes that could make you dance – she had never heard such a ridiculous idea!

All through the night, the little ballerina danced through Annabel's dreams. And when Annabel woke up, she couldn't resist checking at the foot of her bed … even though she was sure there would be nothing there.

But to her astonishment, she found a pair of beautiful dancing shoes, just as the fairy ballerina had promised!

The shoes didn't look very magical, but Annabel couldn't wait to see if they would really work. She slipped them on her feet and stood in the middle of her room, ready to attempt a pirouette. Before she had a chance even to think about what she was doing, she found herself spinning around on the tips of her toes like a real ballerina. She could dance! Unable to believe it, Annabel tried the other steps she had learned in class. She performed them all perfectly.

"What will Miss Carr say?" she giggled, as she spun round and round.

Annabel's dance teacher, Miss Carr, was very impressed with her progress.

"You have been working hard, Annabel," she said at the next class.

"Yes," replied Annabel, smiling to herself. "My nana helped me."

Later that term, Miss Carr took Annabel aside at the end of the lesson.

"I think you are ready to take on one of the lead roles in the show at the end of term," she said. "Would you like to?"

Annabel was overjoyed. "Oh yes!" she cried. "Thank you so much!"

Then she ran off to tell her mother and father the wonderful news.

The following week, Miss Carr announced the show in class. There were mutters of disapproval from some of the older girls when they found out Annabel had the lead role. But Annabel tried not to care what the others thought. She just wanted to dance.

So she worked as hard as she could to learn all the new steps for the show. Of course, the magic shoes made it a lot easier, but Annabel still worked harder than ever before. She wanted every single step to be perfect.

Finally, the day of the show came. Annabel felt nervous and excited all at once. Her parents were coming to watch. Most importantly, Nana would be there, sitting in the front row. Annabel waited in the wings, listening to the auditorium filling up.

She couldn't believe she was going to dance in front of all these people.
"Hurry up Annabel," called Miss Carr, interrupting her thoughts. "It's time to finish getting ready for the show."

Annabel rushed off to the dressing room to find her magic dancing shoes. But when she got there, the shoes were gone! What on earth would she do? How would she ever dance as well as she had with the magic shoes?

Annabel felt tears welling up in her eyes. There was no way she could do the show now. How would she explain herself?

As she sat by herself, wondering what to do, Annabel suddenly felt the tiniest tap on her shoulder. Then there was a little whisper in her ear.
"It's the big show, Annabel. Why are you sitting here crying?"

She rubbed her eyes and looked up to see the fairy ballerina spinning excitedly. "I've been watching you, Annabel, and you really are an amazing dancer," she said."But my magic shoes are gone!" cried Annabel. "I can't dance without them."

The fairy looked over at her and smiled.
"The shoes weren't really magic, Annabel," she said. "The dancing was inside you all along. All you have to do is believe in yourself and you will find that your heart knows every step."
Annabel was shocked. Had it really been her dancing all this time and not the shoes? Maybe she could do the show after all.

Annabel hurried to find Miss Carr and together they went to find a spare pair of dancing shoes in the store wardrobe. Annabel put them on and made her way nervously to the stage. She stood behind the great big curtain, closed her eyes and breathed in deeply. The curtain rose slowly and the music began.

From then on, the evening turned into a blur of spinning, jumping and swirling light and sound. Annabel was lost in the music and dancing.

When the curtain finally came down, Annabel was in a daze. She got changed and went to meet her parents and grandparents at the stage door. Everyone told her how amazing she had been.

"I've never seen you dance better, Annabel," said Nana, giving her a hug. "I'm so proud of you." Then she took her hand and whispered in her ear, "Don't worry, the fairy told me what happened. We'll get you a new pair of dancing shoes for those magic feet of yours."

Annabel could only stare in amazement as her grandmother put a finger to her lips. "And if you keep it a secret," she whispered, "I'll even teach you some new steps."

The Princess Puzzle

Once upon a time, there was a splendid palace where a Princess lived with her parents, the King and Queen. The Princess was a beautiful, happy child and on her next birthday she would inherit the palace and rule the kingdom.

In the days before the Princess' birthday, the palace was buzzing with activity. A huge party had been planned and servants were rushing around the grand ballroom, cleaning, polishing and hanging beautiful decorations. The party was very important, so no expense was spared. All the people in the kingdom were very excited.

Everyone was so busy that they didn't notice the evil sorcerer outside the palace, peering through a window.

"That Princess shall not rule this land," the sorcerer hissed. "I want the kingdom for myself!"

The sorcerer drew a wand from his pocket and muttered a magical spell.

"Magicadabra and magicazane,

Magic two Princesses exactly the same!"

There was a loud BANG and a spray of pink sparks, followed by a puff of smoke. As the smoke cleared, a sly sneer crossed the sorcerer's face. He'd used his magic to create two girls who looked exactly like the Princess! The sorcerer laughed an evil laugh. Now there was no way the kingdom could be passed down to the Princess, because the King and Queen would never know who their real daughter was.

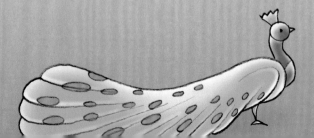

The King nodded his head thoughtfully. "Thank you for your objects," he said to the Princesses. "For tomorrow's task, I will hide an item in the palace that you must bring back to me."

"What will you hide?" the first Princess asked.

"I'm not going to tell you," the King said, "but if you are my daughter, you will know it is something very special to us."

The next day, the Princesses searched the palace for the hidden item.

The first Princess returned with a luxurious string of pearls that belonged to the Queen.

The second Princess handed over an intricately carved goblet.

The third Princess hunted high and low until eventually she found a small thimble hidden under a pillow in one of the bedrooms. The other Princesses sniggered when they saw what she'd chosen to bring. The thimble was worthless.

"Why did you bring this?" the King asked.

The Princess smiled. "When I was a little girl, we used to enjoy playing hunt-the-thimble around the palace. This thimble brings back many special memories for our family."

"I see," the King said. "Now for your final and hardest, task. You must bring us the most precious gift on Earth."

All of the Princesses thought hard about what their precious gift should be.

The first Princess decided on a bag of golden coins, which she piled high in front of the King's throne.

The second Princess chose a chest filled with rubies and sapphires, which she presented to the Queen.

They were both certain that the King and Queen would choose one of them as the Princess. They knew they had performed well in their tasks, much better than the third Princess, who had very little to show for herself.

The third Princess stood in front of the King and Queen, but wasn't carrying anything.

"This is now the second task where you have returned empty-handed," the King said to the third Princess.

"I am not empty-handed," the Princess replied. "You asked us to bring you the most precious gift on Earth. You are my parents and I have brought my love for you. "

The King and Queen looked at each other and smiled. There was no doubt in their minds who their daughter was.

The Queen spoke. "Girls, although you have brought us precious objects and worldly riches, only one of you has demonstrated the kindness, generosity and thoughtfulness of a true Princess." The Queen held out her arms to the third Princess and smiled. "Daughter, we know it's you. You've behaved graciously, as we've always taught you to do. Well done."

As the Queen spoke the words, the sorcerer's spell was broken and the two fake Princesses disappeared in a puff of smoke. The Princess ran to her parents, who hugged her.

The next day, the Princess attended the party to celebrate her birthday. After the crown was placed on the Princess' head, the King, Queen and all the people in the kingdom sang and danced. It was the most joyful celebration the kingdom had ever known.

The Princess and the Peasant Girl

There was once a Princess named Isabella, who was tired of being royal and wished that she could be ordinary. The unhappy Princess could not dance very well and hated attending balls. She got fed up making conversation with the boring dukes and princes that she met. She was uncomfortable in her gowns, because they were tight and stiff. She found it tiresome to sit still for hours while her portrait was painted. But, most of all, she hated the fact that she had to look pretty and behave herself all the time because everyone was always watching her.

By coincidence, a girl called Isobel lived in a nearby village. She had been born on the same day as the Princess and she, too, was unhappy with her life. She was worn out from having to get up at dawn to feed the animals and draw water from the well. She was tired of spending the mornings helping her mother do the laundry and all the other household chores. She wished she could buy her clothes instead of having to make them. But, most of all, she hated the long, boring evenings when there was nothing to do but sew by the dim light of a candle, with only her family for company. Each day, Isobel longed to be a Princess and escape her difficult and dreary life.

One night, at exactly the same moment, just before they fell asleep, Isabella and Isobel both wished that they could change their lives forever. A good fairy heard the girls' wishes and was delighted that, with just one spell, she would be able to help two people at once.

"From their lives let each be free and in each other's bodies be!" chanted the fairy and, with a wave of her magic wand, the spell was cast.

The next morning, Princess Isabella woke with a start. There was something wrong with her bed – it felt hard and lumpy. Then she heard a woman's voice calling her name, but it sounded odd, and it was even stranger for anyone to shout at her. When Isabella opened her eyes and looked around Isobel's simple bedroom with its bare wooden floor, she thought she must be dreaming. The woman was still shouting, so the Princess thought she'd go see what was happening. She put on the worn dress that was hanging from a hook on the bedroom door and made her way downstairs in a daze.

"Hurry up," said Isobel's mother. "You have overslept. The animals are waiting for their food." The Princess stumbled outside. It didn't take her long to find the hungry pigs and hens, who were calling for their breakfast. The Princess fed them grain from a large barrel and went back indoors.

"Where's the water?" asked Isobel's mother.

The Princess had noticed a well in the yard, so she went out and drew a pail of water, just as she'd watched the servant boys in the palace kitchen gardens do. Isobel's mother gave her a strange look when she returned to the kitchen.

"I don't know what's the matter with you today, Isobel," she said. "You look as if you're still half-asleep."

That morning, the Princess followed Isobel's mother's instructions as if she were sleepwalking. After lunch, she had to run some errands in the village. As she walked down the lane to the shops, she remembered that she hadn't even looked in the mirror once. She had been so busy that morning, she hadn't given a thought to her appearance. She wondered what her subjects would say when they saw her wearing such a shabby dress, with her hair in a mess. But, to her great surprise, no one took any notice of her at all.

In the meantime, Isobel had woken up at the palace and she, too, noticed something strange about her bed. It was so soft, she felt as if she were floating on a cloud. She looked around the Princess' bedchamber in amazement, then sat bolt upright. The sun was already high in the sky – she should have fed the animals hours ago! "Your breakfast, your Highness," said a maid, setting down a tray piled high with food and curtseying as she left. Completely bewildered, Isobel ate her breakfast.

A lady-in-waiting arrived with a list of appointments and the day passed in a whirl of activity as everyone prepared for the Royal Ball that was being held at the palace that evening. When it was time to dress for the Ball, Isobel was overwhelmed by the Princess' sparkling jewels and exquisite ballgowns. She chose a beautiful, pink velvet dress with a ruby necklace and matching tiara. Happy that she would not have to get up at dawn the next day, Isobel stayed up later than ever before and danced until her feet ached. As she sank into her goosedown mattress that night, she felt as if all her dreams had come true.

The two girls settled into their new lives. Each afternoon, Isabella walked to the village, where she went about her business without being stared at all the time. She loved chatting to the people and, for the first time in her life, she knew that they weren't being nice to her just because she was a Princess. She enjoyed the simple, fresh food eaten at the kitchen table with Isobel's large and cheerful family far more than the lonely meals in her royal apartments, or the formal banquets, where her dresses were so tight, she could hardly breathe, let alone eat.

At the palace, Isobel took delight in her beautiful gowns and splendid surroundings. After years of looking after the animals and doing the household chores, she enjoyed having servants to take care of her every need. She adored going to balls and dancing all night and she loved the attention of all the dukes and princes she met.